*European Agreement Concerning the Work of Crews of Vehicles Engaged in Intl' Road Transport*  
24-8-20

CPC Drivers Training Manual

Drivers' hours and tachographs: goods vehicles

## Contents

**EU and AETR rules on drivers' hours** ............................ 10

**Introduction** ............................ 10

    **Which rules apply** ............................ 11

1. EU and AETR rules on drivers' hours ............................ 14

    **Exemptions and derogations** ............................ 15

        **Exemptions** ............................ 15

        European Commission special authorisation exemptions ............................ 19

        Derogations ............................ 20

        Concession for members of a volunteer force and instructors in the Cadet Corps ............... 29

    **Driving** ............................ 32

CPC Drivers Training Manual

**Breaks and driving limits** ................................................................................................ 32
    **Daily driving limit** ............................................................................................... 38
    **Weekly driving limit** ........................................................................................... 40
**Daily rest periods** ........................................................................................................... 45
    **Multi-manning** ..................................................................................................... 49
    **Journeys involving ferry or train transport** ...................................................... 53
    **Being on call during a daily rest period** .......................................................... 55
**Weekly rest periods** ....................................................................................................... 57
    **Being on call during a weekly rest period** ...................................................... 62
**Emergencies** ................................................................................................................... 63
**Travelling time** ............................................................................................................... 64
**Unforeseen events** ......................................................................................................... 65
**Summary of EU limits on drivers' hours** ..................................................................... 66
    **Breaks from driving** ............................................................................................ 67

| | |
|---|---|
| **Daily driving** | 67 |
| **Weekly driving** | 67 |
| **Two-weekly driving** | 67 |
| **Daily rest** | 68 |
| **Multi-manning daily rest** | 68 |
| **Ferry/train daily rest** | 68 |
| **Weekly rest** | 69 |
| **AETR rules** | 69 |
| **Working Time Regulations** | 70 |
| 2. Great Britain domestic rules | 71 |
| **Overview** | 71 |
| **Domestic rules exemptions** | 71 |
| **Domestic driving limits** | 72 |
| **Daily driving** | 72 |

| | |
|---|---:|
| **Daily duty** | 72 |
| **Record keeping** | 74 |
| **Exemptions from keeping records** | 75 |
| **Emergencies** | 75 |
| **Records for vehicles carrying postal articles** | 76 |
| **Travelling abroad** | 76 |
| **Mixed vehicle types** | 77 |
| **Working Time Regulations** | 77 |
| 3. Mixed EU/AETR and Great Britain domestic driving | 78 |
| 4. Tachograph rules | 82 |
| **Overview** | 82 |
| **Analogue tachographs** | 84 |
| **Charts and records** | 84 |
| **Centrefield entries** | 88 |

| | |
|---|---|
| **Manual entries** | 89 |
| **Digital tachographs** | 98 |
|     Driver cards and records | 98 |
|     How to apply for driver cards | 102 |
|     Lost, stolen or malfunctioning driver cards | 103 |
|     UTC – the time set on a digital tachograph | 104 |
|     Manual records | 105 |
| **Common rules** | 107 |
|     Operation of the mode switch or button | 107 |
|     Multi-manning – second driver record | 109 |
|     Travelling time | 109 |
|     Mixed records – analogue and digital equipment | 110 |
|     Recording other work | 110 |
|     Information to operators | 111 |

## CPC Drivers Training Manual

- **Rest and other days off** ............... 112
- **Responsibilities of operators** ............... 112
  - **Tachograph calibration and inspection** ............... 116
  - **Breakdown of equipment** ............... 117
  - **Digital tachographs – company cards** ............... 118

## 5. Enforcement and penalties ............... 121

- **Enforcement powers and sanctions** ............... 121
- **Powers** ............... 121
- **Sanctions** ............... 122
  - **Verbal warnings** ............... 122
  - **Offence rectification notice** ............... 122
  - **Prohibition** ............... 123
  - **Fixed penalties and deposits** ............... 123
  - **Prosecution** ............... 124

## CPC Drivers Training Manual

    **Referral to the Traffic Commissioner** .................................................................. 124

**Infringements of GB domestic drivers' hours rules** ............................................... 125

**Infringements of the EU drivers' hours rules** ....................................................... 125

**EU rules: co-liability** ............................................................................................. 127

**Penalties for infringements of the drivers' hours rules in Great Britain** ............... 129

    **Maximum fines** ................................................................................................ 129

## Annex 1. Legislation .................................................................................................. 131

    **EU rules** ............................................................................................................ 131

    **AETR rules** ....................................................................................................... 133

    **Domestic rules** .................................................................................................. 133

## Annex 2. Working time rules .................................................................................... 134

    **Driving under the EU drivers' hours rules** ....................................................... 134

    **Driving under the GB domestic drivers' hours rules (or are an occasional mobile worker)** .. 137

## Annex 3. Example Sheet ............................................................................................ 139

**Further information** ................................................................................................ 140

**Definition of a self-employed driver under the 2005 Regulations** ......................... 141

**Definition of an occasional mobile worker under the 2005 Regulations** ............... 141

**Definition of self-employed under the 1998 Regulations** ....................................... 142

CPC Drivers Training Manual

## CPC Drivers Training Tachograph Manual

Find us on Facebook @CPCdriverstraining

cpcsales@post.com

EU and AETR rules on drivers' hours

How the EU drivers' hours rules for goods vehicles work.

CPC Drivers Training Manual

# UK Drivers' hours and tachographs: goods vehicles

# EU and AETR rules on drivers' hours

How the EU drivers' hours rules for goods vehicles work.

## Introduction

This guide provides advice to drivers and operators of goods vehicles, whether used privately or commercially. It explains the rules for drivers' hours and the keeping of records, and updates previous guidance from 2011. The EU regulations also place a responsibility on others in the supply chain such as consignors, freight forwarders, contractors, sub-contractors and driver agencies. People working in these sectors of the road haulage industry may benefit from an understanding of the guidance offered here.

Those who are involved in international operations are advised to check whether the other country or countries in which they operate produce equivalent guidance. CPC Drivers Training recommends that you contact the relevant embassy.

As with any legislation, previous and future court judgments may assist interpretation on a particular point. Where significant court judgments on interpretation are relevant, these have been incorporated in the text. Some important judgments are available – many in shortened form – in legal reference books held by larger reference libraries. If you are in doubt as to how these rules apply to you, seek your own legal advice.

## Which rules apply

Within Great Britain (GB), either GB domestic or EU rules may apply. For international journeys, either the EU rules or the European Agreement Concerning the Work of Crews of Vehicles Engaged in International Road Transport (AETR) may apply. Which set of rules applies depends on the type of driving and the type of vehicle being used, and, in the case of international journeys, the countries to be visited.

Most vehicles used for the carriage of goods by road and with a maximum permissible weight (including any trailer or semi-trailer) of over 3.5 tonnes are in scope of the EU rules. 'Carriage by road' is defined as any journey entirely or in part made on roads open to the public of a vehicle, laden or unladen, used for the carriage of passengers or goods. 'Off-road' driving is in scope where it forms part of a journey that also takes place on public roads. Journeys made that are entirely 'off-road' are out of scope of the EU rules.

International journeys to or through countries that are outside the EU but are signatories to the AETR are subject to AETR rules.

**International journey** An international journey means a journey to or from another EU member state, including the part of the journey within the UK.

For journeys that are partly in the EU and partly in countries that are neither in the EU nor signatories to AETR, EU rules will apply to that portion of the journey that is in the EU. Countries outside the EU and AETR are likely to have their own regulations governing drivers' hours, which should be adhered to while you are driving in that country.

CPC Drivers Training Manual

Vehicles that are exempted from the EU rules come under GB domestic rules on drivers' hours while engaged in domestic journeys.

CPC Drivers Training Manual

## 1. EU and AETR rules on drivers' hours

The EU rules (Regulation (EC) 561/2006) apply to drivers of most vehicles used for the carriage of goods - defined as goods or burden of any description - (including dual purpose vehicles) where the maximum permissible weight of the vehicle, including any trailer or semi-trailer, exceeds 3.5 tonnes and where the vehicle is used within the UK or between the UK and other EU and EEA countries and Switzerland. It is however not necessary for a vehicle to be laden for it to be in scope of the EC/ AETR rules.

Vehicle operations that take place off the public road or vehicles that are never used to carry goods on a public road are out of scope.

Additionally drivers who are employed to drive vehicles which would normally be in scope of EU/ AETR rules but who never carry goods or passengers in the course of that employment are not considered to be within scope of the regulations. For example, this covers operations such as:

- driving a hire vehicle for the purpose of delivery or collection
- empty vehicles being driven to or from annual test or a place of repair

- driving a vehicle for the purpose of moving it between depots
- driving a new/demonstrator vehicle for the purpose of collection or delivery
- vehicles being driven to be scrapped

A 'driver' is anyone who drives a vehicle or is carried on the vehicle in order to be available for driving.

# Exemptions and derogations

The following table contains a list of vehicles or uses that are exempt from the EU rules regardless of where the vehicle is driven within the EU. See also 'Unforeseen events'.

In some cases it may be necessary to refer to case law for definitive interpretations.

## Exemptions

**Vehicles not capable of exceeding 40 km/ h**

For example, some works vehicles fall into this category. Also includes vehicles incapable of exceeding 40 km/ h by virtue of a set speed limiter.

**Vehicles owned or hired without a driver by the Armed Forces, civil defence services, fire services and forces responsible for maintaining public order, when the carriage is undertaken as a consequence of the tasks assigned to these services and is under their control.**

Does not apply to commercial operators contracted by these bodies.

**Vehicles, including vehicles used in the non-commercial transport of humanitarian aid, used in emergencies or rescue operations.**

The EU rules do not define an 'emergency' but we consider this would certainly include any of the situations that would be considered an emergency for the purposes of the GB domestic drivers' hours legislation, namely a situation where immediate preventative action is needed to avoid:

- danger to the life or health of people or animals
- serious interruption of essential public services (gas, water, electricity or drainage), of telecommunication and postal services, or in the use of roads, railways, ports or airports or
- serious damage to property

Vehicles used in connection with emergency or rescue operations would be exempt from the EU rules for the duration of the emergency.

The important aspect of humanitarian aid is that it only applies to transport carried out on a non-commercial basis e.g. transportation of donated clothes, food parcels etc. The aid supplied must however be in direct response to an emergency or rescue operation.

**Specialised vehicles used for medical purposes.**

For example, mobile chest x-ray units.

**Specialised breakdown vehicles operating within a 100 km radius of their base.**

'Specialised breakdown vehicle' was interpreted by the European Court as a vehicle whose construction, fitments and other permanent characteristics were such that it would be used mainly for removing vehicles that had recently been involved in an accident or broken down.

**Vehicles undergoing road tests for technical development, repair or maintenance purposes, and new or rebuilt vehicles which have not yet been put into service.**

This doesn't apply to vehicles normally falling in scope of EU rules but which are on journeys to or from testing stations for the purposes of an annual test.

**Vehicles or combinations of vehicles with a maximum permissible mass not exceeding 7.5 tonnes used for the non-commercial carriage of goods.**

Examples could include a person moving house and goods carried by a non-profit making group or registered charity.

European Court of Justice case law provides that the term non-commercial also applies to the carriage of goods by a private individual for their own purposes purely as part of a hobby where that hobby is in part financed by financial contributions from external persons or undertakings and where no payment is made for the carriage of goods per se.

**Commercial vehicles that have a historic status according to the legislation of the Member State in which they are driven and that are used for the non-commercial carriage of goods.**

In GB, a vehicle is a historic vehicle if it was manufactured more than 25 years before the occasion on which it is being driven.

**Vehicles or combinations of vehicles with a maximum permissible mass not exceeding 7.5 tonnes that are used for carrying materials, equipment or machinery for the driver's use in the course of their work and which are used only within a 100 km radius from the base of the undertaking and on the condition that driving the vehicle does not constitute the driver's main activity.**

This would apply to tradesmen such as electricians or builders carrying tools or materials for their own use.

### European Commission special authorisation exemptions

The following vehicles are exempt from the EU rules in Great Britain (England, Scotland and Wales) after the European Commission granted a special authorisation:

- any vehicle which is being used by the Royal National Lifeboat Institution
- any vehicle that was manufactured before 1 January 1947
- any vehicle that is propelled by steam

CPC Drivers Training Manual

## Derogations

The EU rules grant Member States the power to apply derogations to further specific categories of vehicles and drivers while on national only journeys. The following derogations have been implemented in the UK.

In some cases it may be necessary to refer to case law for definitive interpretations.

**Vehicles owned or hired without a driver by public authorities that do not compete with private transport undertakings.**

The derogation only applies to vehicles being used:

- for the provision of ambulance services by or at the request of an NHS body
- for the transport of organs, blood, equipment, medical supplies or personnel by or at the request of an NHS body
- by a local authority to provide services for old people or for mentally or physically handicapped people or
- by HM Coastguard or a general or local lighthouse authority
- for maintaining railways by:

- the British Railways Board
- any holder of a network licence which is a company wholly owned by the Crown
- Transport for London (or a wholly owned subsidiary)
- a Passenger Transport Executive
- a local authority
- by the British Waterways Board for the purpose of maintaining navigable waterways

**Vehicles used or hired without a driver by agricultural, horticultural, forestry, farming or fishery undertakings for carrying goods as part of their own entrepreneurial activity within a radius of 100 km from the base of the undertaking.**

This applies only to those who are an undertaking related to (ie in the business of) the activities of agricultural, horticultural, forestry, farming or fishery and are transporting goods in relation to that business. If an organisation has a division for one of the listed activities then the derogation would apply only to that division. If an organisation as a whole is neither an undertaking, nor has a separate division relating to the listed activities, but it nonetheless operates vehicles occasionally for such purposes the derogation would not apply to its use of vehicles for those occasional purposes.

For a vehicle used by a horticulture undertaking, the derogation would apply to the carriage of goods relating to the small-scale management of non built-up land and which have a tangible link to horticulture so would include the carriage of plants, hard landscaping and fencing materials and related tools.

For a vehicle used by fishery undertakings, the derogation only applies if it is being used to carry live fish or to carry a catch of fish from the place of landing to a place where it is to be processed. The term 'fish' includes finfish and shellfish.

**Agricultural tractors and forestry tractors used for agricultural or forestry activities within a 100 km radius from the base of the undertaking that owns, hires or leases the tractor.**

**Vehicles that are used to carry live animals between a farm and a market or from a market to a slaughterhouse where the distance between the farm and the market or between the market and the slaughterhouse does not exceed 100 km.**

**Vehicles being used to carry animal waste or carcasses that are not intended for human consumption.**

The derogation applies to carriage of animal waste or carcasses, including fallen stock, from farms and abattoirs. "Animal waste" is deemed to be a substance or object that is discarded or is intended or required to be discarded and a "carcass" to mean the body of a dead animal. The derogation doesn't apply to animal derived products nor to waste from supermarkets, shops etc.

**Specially fitted mobile project vehicles, the primary purpose of which is use as an educational facility when stationary.**

For example play buses and mobile libraries.

**Vehicles or combinations of vehicles with a maximum permissible mass not exceeding 7.5 tonnes.**

This refers to those that are used by universal service providers as defined in Article 2(13) of Directive 96/67/EC of the European Parliament and of the Council of 15 December 1997 on common rules for the development of the internal market of Community postal services and the improvement of quality service to deliver items as part of the universal service.

These vehicles shall be used only within a 100 km radius of the base of the undertaking and on the condition that driving the vehicle does not constitute the driver's main activity.

Currently the only universal service provider in the UK is the Royal Mail. Universal service provider vehicles must have a tachograph fitted.

**Vehicles operated exclusively on islands whose area does not exceed 2,300 square kilometres and that are not linked to the rest of Great Britain by a bridge, ford or tunnel open for use by a motor vehicle.**

**Vehicles used for the carriage of goods within a 100 km radius from the base of the undertaking and propelled by means of natural or liquefied gas or electricity, the maximum permissible mass of which, including the mass of a trailer or semi-trailer, does not exceed 7.5 tonnes.**

**Vehicles used for driving instruction and examination with a view to obtaining a driving licence or a certificate of professional competence, provided that they are not being used for the commercial carriage of goods or passengers**

Includes instruction for renewal of Driver Certificate of Professional Competence (CPC).

**Vehicles used in connection with sewerage, flood protection, water, gas and electricity maintenance services, road maintenance or control, door-to-door household refuse collection or disposal, telegraph or telephone services, radio or television broadcasting and the detection of radio or television transmitters or receivers.**

There have been a number of significant court rulings from the European Court of Justice and British courts dealing with this exemption. Common themes have included a direct and close involvement in the exempt activity; the principle of a general service in the public interest; and the limited and secondary nature of the transport activity.

It's DVSA's view that vehicles used in connection with sewerage, flood protection, water, gas and electricity services must be involved in the maintenance of an existing service (rather than the construction of a new service) to claim the concession.

For vehicles used in connection with sewerage maintenance services the term "maintenance" also applies to the removal of waste from a system but only where the waste is removed directly onto the vehicle and immediately taken away for treatment. This would also include transporting partially treated sewage from satellite sites to main sites.

CPC Drivers Training Manual

The derogation doesn't apply to the movement of sewage sludge which has been treated to make a product which is then used for another purpose such as, for example, fertiliser.

The types of refuse collection and disposal operations likely to be exempt are:

- the door-to-door collection or from communal waste points of domestic waste such as black bin bags, green waste, garden waste, newspapers or glass from households
- the collection of sofas and household appliances from households within a local area
- the clearing of a home following a bereavement, provided refuse collection and disposal is the core purpose

The derogation will also apply to the collection of the domestic type waste from commercial premises but would not extend to collecting commercial waste, for example, waste generated by a manufacturing process.

Vehicles used in connection with road maintenance services which:

- are engaged on a journey directly relating to the maintenance services, for example, removing rubble or other materials or
- are being used directly on the maintenance activity, for example, laying tarmac

These will fall within this derogation however journeys to a site for the purpose of positioning the vehicle in readiness for engaging in the maintenance activity or for returning to base after the maintenance activity has ended will not fall within this derogation.

Vehicles which are to be used or have been used that same day in connection with highway maintenance and control and don't travel far from the site where the work of highway maintenance is being carried out will fall within the derogation.

**Specialised vehicles transporting circus and funfair equipment.**

A recent court judgment determined that in order for catering vehicles or trailers to be able to use this derogation they must be specialised.

In the case of a specialised trailer, it isn't necessary for the drawing vehicle to also be specialised. This means that a vehicle towing a catering/refreshment trailer would be deemed to be specialised as the trailer itself is specialised. However, a vehicle or trailer without any special features for carrying (rather than towing) a catering kiosk wouldn't be deemed to be specialised.

A vehicle (with or without a trailer) transporting catering kiosks or any other equipment used for a purpose directly connected to a circus or funfair which is going to, for example, a local market, car boot sale, sporting event, shopping centre car park etc would not be entitled to claim this derogation.

Being a member of a guild or association (such as the Showman's Guild or the Circus Proprietors Association) does not in itself give exemption to the EC drivers' hours requirements as the equipment carried must still be funfair or circus equipment.

**Vehicles used for milk collection from farms or the return to farms of milk containers or milk products intended for animal feed.**

**Vehicles used exclusively on roads inside hub facilities such as ports, airports, interports and railway terminals.**

This applies only to those vehicles being used within the perimeter of these areas (rather than those driving to or through the areas), although we accept that these vehicles may occasionally leave the site for vehicle maintenance purposes.

## Concession for members of a volunteer force and instructors in the Cadet Corps

There is also a concession in place from the daily and weekly rest requirements specified in the EU drivers' hours regulations for professional drivers who are also members of a volunteer reserve force (e.g the Army Reserve) or are an instructor in the Cadet Corps.

The conditions of the concession are:

- a suspension of the requirement to take a daily rest period within a period of 24 hours when the driver commenced the weekly training as a reservist or as an instructor in the cadet corps
- a suspension of the requirement to take a weekly rest period at the end of the six 24 hour periods from the previous weekly rest period when the driver commences their driving as a reservist or as an instructor in the cadet corps
- a regular daily rest must still be taken before they start work for their primary employer and a regular weekly rest must be taken no later than at the end of the sixth day following training
- the exception is limited to a maximum of:
    - 10 weekend training sessions and

CPC Drivers Training Manual

- - fifteen days' annual camp training in any year
- drivers must not attend weekend training sessions on any two consecutive weekends
- drivers must not attend any annual camp training that takes place over the weekend that immediately follows a weekend training session that the driver has attended
- drivers must not attend a weekend training session on the weekend that immediately follows any annual camp training that the driver has attended
- drivers must not attend any annual camp training that takes place over the weekend that immediately follows the end of an earlier period of annual camp training that the driver has attended
- a regular daily rest period of at least eleven hours must be taken immediately following the end of each weekend training session and at the end of each period of annual camp training
- a regular weekly rest period of a least forty-five hours must be taken no later than the end of the sixth day following the end of the day on which a weekend training session or, as the case may be, a period of annual camp training ends

No such concessions are available for those undertaking retained fire and rescue work or volunteer police work so activities of that nature can only be undertaken if they do not impact on legally required daily and weekly rest periods or if the situation is deemed to be an emergency as detailed <u>Emergencies</u>.

CPC Drivers Training Manual

If it is exempt from the EU rules due to the provisions listed above then the vehicle will usually be in scope of the GB domestic rules when travelling in GB - see GB domestic rules.

# Driving

'Driving time' is the duration of driving activity recorded either by the recording equipment or manually when the recording equipment is broken.

Even a short period of driving under EU rules during any day by a driver will mean that they are in scope of the EU rules for the whole of that day and must comply with the daily driving, break and rest requirements; they will also have to comply with the weekly rest requirement and driving limit.

# Breaks and driving limits

### Breaks

After a driving period of no more than 4.5 hours, a driver must immediately take a break of at least 45 minutes unless they take a rest period. A break taken in this way must not be interrupted.

CPC Drivers Training Manual

For example:

| 4.5 hrs | 45 mins |

| 2.5 hrs | 1 hr | 2 hrs | 45 mins |

33

**A break** A break is any period during which a driver may not carry out any driving or any other work and which is used exclusively for recuperation. A break may be taken in a moving vehicle, provided no other work is undertaken.

Alternatively, a full 45 minute break can be replaced by one break of at least 15 minutes followed by another break of at least 30 minutes. These breaks must be distributed over the 4.5 hour period. Breaks of less than 15 minutes will not contribute towards a qualifying break, but neither will they be counted as duty or driving time. The EU rules will only allow a split-break pattern that shows the second period of break being at least 30 minutes, such as in the

following examples:

| 2 hrs | 15 mins | 2.5 hrs | 30 mins |

CPC Drivers Training Manual

| 2 hrs | 34 mins | 2.5 hrs | 30 mins |
|---|---|---|---|

| 2 hrs | 30 mins | 2.5 hrs | 15 mins | |
|---|---|---|---|---|

CPC Drivers Training Manual

| 2 hrs | 30 mins | 2.5 hrs | 15 mins | |
|---|---|---|---|---|

The above split-break pattern is illegal because the second break is less than 30 minutes.

A driver 'wipes the slate clean' if they take a 45 minute break (or qualifying breaks totalling 45 minutes before or at the end of a 4.5 hour driving period. This means that the next 4.5 hour driving period begins with the completion of that qualifying break, and in assessing break requirements for the new 4.5 hour period, no reference is to be made to driving time accumulated before this point.

CPC Drivers Training Manual

For example:

| 1.5 hrs | 15 mins | 1.5 hrs | 30 mins | 4.5 hours | 45 mins |

Breaks may also be required under the separate Road Transport (Working Time) Regulations 2005. See Annex 2 for further details.

CPC Drivers Training Manual

## Daily driving limit

The maximum daily driving time is 9 hours; for example:

| 4.5 hrs | 45 mins | 4.5 hrs |
|---------|---------|---------|

| 2 hrs | 45 mins | 4.5 hrs | 45 mins | 2.5 hrs |
|-------|---------|---------|---------|---------|

The maximum daily driving time can be increased to 10 hours twice in a fixed week;

CPC Drivers Training Manual

for example:

| 4.5 hrs | 45 mins | 4.5 hrs | 45 mins | 1 hr |
|---|---|---|---|---|

| 2 hrs | 45 mins | 4.5 hrs | 45 mins | 3.5 hrs |
|---|---|---|---|---|

**Daily driving time** Daily driving time is either:

- the total accumulated driving time between the end of one daily rest period and the beginning of the following daily rest period
- the total accumulated driving time between a daily rest period and a weekly rest period (or vice versa)

Note: All off road driving between rest periods will also count towards the daily driving limit where there is also driving on the public highway between those same rest periods. Where there is no driving on the public highway between rest periods then any off road driving is considered to be 'other work'.

## Weekly driving limit

The maximum weekly driving limit is 56 hours, which applies to a fixed week.

**A fixed week** A fixed week starts at 00.00 on Monday and ends at 24.00 on the following Sunday.

The following diagram shows an example of how this might be achieved:

| Sun | Weekly rest |
|---|---|
| Mon | 9 hours driving |
| Tues | 10 hours driving |
| Wed | 9 hours driving |
| Thu | 9 hours driving |
| Fri | 10 hours driving |
| Sat | 9 hours driving |
| Sun | Weekly rest |

Total weekly hours = (4 x 9) + (2 x 10) = 56.

CPC Drivers Training Manual

**Two-weekly driving limit**

The maximum driving time over any two-weekly period is 90 hours; for example:

| Week | Total hours of driving | Two-weekly totals |
|---|---|---|
| 9  | 56 hours | 90 hours |
| 10 | 34 hours | 79 hours |
| 11 | 45 hours | 90 hours |
| 12 | 45 hours | 88 hours |
| 13 | 43 hours | |

CPC Drivers Training Manual

The following is an example of how a driver's duties might be organised in compliance with the rules on weekly and two-weekly driving limits:

CPC Drivers Training Manual

| | | | Weekly | Two weeks | Between weekly rests |
|---|---|---|---|---|---|
| Mon | Driving 9 hours | Daily rest | Total 56 hours driving during fixed week 1 | Total 90 hours driving during fixed weeks 1 and 2 | Total 58 hours driving between weekly rests |
| Tue | Driving 9 hours | Daily rest | | | |
| Wed | Driving 9 hours | Daily rest | | | |
| Thu | Weekly rest (reduced) | | | | |
| Fri | Driving 10 hours | Daily rest | | | |
| Sat | Driving 10 hours | Daily rest | | | |
| Sun | Driving 9 hours | Daily rest | | | |
| Mon | Driving 9 hours | Daily rest | Total 34 hours driving during fixed week 2 | | |
| Tues | Driving 10 hours | Daily rest | | | |
| Wed | Driving 10 hours | Daily rest | | | |
| Thu | Weekly rest | | | | |
| Fri | Weekly rest | | | | |
| Sat | Compensation | | | | |
| Sun | Driving 5 hours | Daily rest | | | |

## Daily rest periods

A driver must take a daily rest period within each period of 24 hours after the end of the previous daily or weekly rest period. An 11 hour (or more) daily rest is called a regular daily rest period.

**A rest** A rest is an uninterrupted period where a driver may freely dispose of their time.

Time spent working in other employment or under obligation or instruction, regardless of the occupation type, cannot be counted as rest. This includes work where you are self-employed, work related to community service, non-emergency retained fire fighting, or training related to obtaining/retaining a Driver Certificate of Professional Competence (CPC) where the training is at the request or instigation of an employer. Driver CPC training can only be undertaken during rest periods where the driver is attending voluntarily and not at the request of the employer.

CPC Drivers Training Manual

For information on emergency situations please go to Emergencies

| 24 hour period ||
| Driving | Breaks | Other work | Regular daily rest |
|---|---|
| 13 hours | 11 hours |

Alternatively, a driver can split a regular daily rest period into two periods. The first period must be at least 3 hours of uninterrupted rest and can be taken at any time during the day. The second must be at least 9 hours of uninterrupted rest, giving a total minimum rest of 12 hours.

For example:

| 24 hr period |||||
|---|---|---|---|---|
| Driving / Breaks / Other work | Rest | Driving / Breaks / Other work | Rest ||
| 8 hrs | 3 hrs | 4 hrs | 9 hrs ||

A driver may reduce their daily rest period to no less than 9 continuous hours, but this can be done no more than three times between any two weekly rest periods; no compensation for the reduction is required. A daily rest that is less than 11 hours but at least 9 hours long is called a reduced daily rest period.

| 24 hour period |||||
|---|---|---|---|---|
| Driving | Breaks | Other work | Reduced daily rest ||
| 15 hours ||| 9 hours ||

When a daily rest is taken, this may be taken in a vehicle, as long as it has suitable sleeping facilities and is stationary.

**Suitable sleeping facilities** We consider suitable sleeping facilities to be a bunk or other type of bed which is primarily designed for sleeping on. Sleeping on or across seats does not meet the requirement of suitable facilities. If a vehicle has no suitable sleeping facilities then other arrangements, for example guest house or hotel accommodation, should be used.

CPC Drivers Training Manual

To summarise, a driver who begins work at 06.00 on day 1 must, by 06.00 on day 2 at the latest, have completed either:

- a regular daily rest period of at least 11 hours or
- a split regular daily rest period of at least 12 hours or
- if entitled a reduced daily rest period of at least 9 hours

**Regular daily rest** A continuous period of at least 11 hours' rest.

**Split daily rest period** A regular rest taken in two separate periods – the first at least 3 hours, and the second at least 9 hours.

**Reduced daily rest period** A continuous rest period of at least 9 hours but less than 11 hours.

## Multi-manning

'Multi-manning' is the situation where, during each period of driving between any two consecutive daily rest periods, or between a daily rest period and a weekly rest period, there are at least two drivers in the vehicle to do the driving. For the first hour of multi-manning the presence of another driver or drivers is optional, but for the remainder of the period it is compulsory. This allows for a vehicle to depart from its operating centre and collect a second driver along the way, providing that this is done within 1 hour of the first driver starting work.

Where the above conditions are complied with then the multi-manning concession may be used – that is each driver must have a daily rest period of at least 9 consecutive hours but they may do so within the 30-hour period that starts at the end of the last daily or weekly rest period (rather than the normal 24 hour period).

If however the conditions cannot be complied with, then drivers sharing duties on a journey will individually be governed by single manning rules and will not be able to use the concession which allows daily rest to be taken in a 30 hour period.

Organising drivers' duties in such a fashion enables a crew's duties to be spread over 21 hours however where a driver utilises the multi-manning daily rest concession (of 9 hours rest in a 30 hour period) that rest period cannot be counted as a regular daily rest as it is of less than 11 hours duration. These rest periods therefore count towards the limit of 3 reduced rest periods between any 2 consecutive weekly rest periods.

Drivers engaged on multi-manning can however, if they choose, take either:

- a split daily rest within the 30 hour period so long as it taken as the first period being at least 3 hours and the second period being at least 9 hours
- a rest period of at least 11 hours in the 30 hour period

Both of these options are regular daily rest period and so would not count towards the limit of three reduced daily rest period between weekly rest periods.

This is an example of how the duties of a two-man crew could be organised to take maximum advantage of multi-manning daily rest concession:

# CPC Drivers Training Manual

|  | Driver 1 | Driver 2 |
|---|---|---|
| **30 hour period** | Daily rest | Daily rest |
|  | Other work 1 hour | Daily rest (not on vehicle) 1 hour |
|  | Driving 4.5 hours | Availability 4.5 hours |
|  | Break + availability 4.5 hours | Driving 4.5 hours |
|  | Driving 4.5 hours | Break + availability 4.5 hours |
|  | Break + availability 4.5 hours | Driving 4.5 hours |
|  | Driving 1 hour | Break + availability 1 hour |
|  | Break 1 hour | Driving 1 hour |
|  | Daily rest 9 hours | Daily rest 9 hours |

The maximum driving time for a two-man crew taking advantage of this concession is 20 hours before a daily rest is required (although only if both drivers are entitled to drive 10 hours).

Under multi-manning, the 'second' driver in a crew may not necessarily be the same driver for the duration of the first driver's shift but could in principle be any number of drivers as long as the conditions are met. Whether these second drivers could claim the multi-manning concession in these circumstances would depend on their other duties.

On a multi-manning operation, 45 minutes of a period of availability will be considered to be a break, so long as the co-driver does no work.

Other than the daily rest concession detailed above drivers engaged in multi-manning are governed by the same rules that apply to single-manned vehicles.

## Journeys involving ferry or train transport

Where a driver accompanies a vehicle that is being transported by ferry or train, the daily rest requirements are more flexible.

A regular daily rest period, that is one of 11 hours duration or 12 hours if split, may be interrupted no more than twice, but the total interruption must not exceed 1 hour in total. This allows for a vehicle to be driven on to a ferry and off again at the end of the crossing. Where

CPC Drivers Training Manual

the rest period is interrupted in this way, the total accumulated rest period must still be at least 11 hours or 12 hours if split. A bunk or couchette must be available during the rest period.

Drivers who are engaged on multi-manning can also interrupt a rest period however they may only do so where the rest period in the 30 hour spreadover is a regular daily rest of at least 11 hours or 12 hours if it is a split daily rest.

Any rest that is interrupted must be completed within the 24 hour period (if single manned) or within the 30 hours period (if multi-manned). The 24 or 30 hour period commences at the point of starting duty following the end of a daily or weekly rest period.

For example, a qualifying regular daily rest period could be interrupted in the following manner:

| 2 hrs | 30 mins (embarkation) | 7 hrs (on ferry or train) | 30 mins (disembarkation) | 2 hrs |

For example, a split daily rest could be interrupted in the following manner:

| 30 mins | 3 hrs | 30 mins | 9 hrs (start) | 20 mins (embarkation) | 9 hrs (cont) | 35 mins (disembarkation) | 9 hrs (end) |
|---|---|---|---|---|---|---|---|

It is also permitted to have one of the interruption periods falling in the 3 hour part of the split rest period and one interruption period falling in the 9 hour part of the split rest period or for both parts of the interruption period to fall within the 3 hour part of the split daily rest.

## Being on call during a daily rest period

Drivers who are on call during any period of legally required rest must at all times be able to dispose of the rest time as they choose. This means that an employer cannot impose any limitations on drivers during such periods, for example requiring them to remain in or close to home or at another location. Drivers must be able to dispose of their free time as they choose (but this does not include undertaking any work where they are under the control of or are fulfilling an obligation to an employer). Being on call may only extend as far as a driver agreeing to answer a call during a rest period but only if the driver so chooses. On receiving a call to return to work drivers may only do so if they have completed the legally required amount of rest or if the work is deemed to be an emergency See <u>Emergencies</u>.

## Weekly rest periods

A driver must start a weekly rest period no later than at the end of six consecutive 24-hour periods from the end of the last weekly rest period.

| Week 1 | | Week 2 | | Week 3 |
|---|---|---|---|---|
| Rest 45 hours | 144 hours | Rest 45 hours | 80 hours | Rest 45 hours |

A regular weekly rest period is a period of at least 45 consecutive hours.

**A weekly rest period** A weekly rest period is the weekly period during which drivers may freely dispose of their time. It may be either a 'regular weekly rest period' or a 'reduced weekly rest period'.

CPC Drivers Training Manual

Time spent working in other employment or under obligation or instruction, regardless of the occupation type, cannot be counted as rest. This includes work where you are self-employed, work related to community service, non-emergency* retained fire fighting, or training related to obtaining/retaining Driver CPC where the training is at the request or instigation of an employer. Driver CPC training can only be undertaken during rest periods where the driver is attending voluntarily.

*For work related to emergencies please go to Emergencies

Note: An actual working week starts at the end of a weekly rest period, and finishes when another weekly rest period is commenced, which may mean that weekly rest is taken in the middle of a fixed (Monday–Sunday) week. This is perfectly acceptable – the working week is not required to be aligned with the 'fixed' week defined in the rules, provided all the relevant limits are complied with.

Alternatively, a driver can take a reduced weekly rest period of a minimum of 24 consecutive hours. If a reduction is taken, it must be compensated for by an equivalent period of rest taken in one block before the end of the third week following the week in question. The compensating rest must be attached to a period of rest of at least 9 hours – in effect either a weekly or a daily rest period.

For example, where a driver reduces a weekly rest period to 33 hours in week 1, they must compensate for this by attaching a 12-hour period of rest to another rest period of at least 9 hours before the end of week 4. This compensation cannot be taken in several smaller periods. (See example below.)

| Weekly rest | | | |
|---|---|---|---|
| Week 1 | Week 2 | Week 3 | Week 4 |
| 33 hrs | 45 hrs | 45 hrs | 45 hrs + 12 hrs compensation |

**A regular weekly rest period** A regular weekly rest is a period of rest of at least 45 hours' duration.

**A reduced weekly rest period** A reduced weekly rest is a rest period of at least 24 but less than 45 hours' duration.

CPC Drivers Training Manual

In any two consecutive 'fixed' weeks a driver must take at least:

- 2 regular weekly rests or
- one regular weekly rest and one reduced weekly rest

Other weekly rests of any type may be taken in any 2 consecutive 'fixed weeks' in addition to this minimum requirement.

The following tables are examples of how a driver's duties might be organised in compliance with the rules on weekly rest, which allow two reduced weekly rest periods to be taken consecutively. This complies with the rules because at least one regular and one reduced weekly rest period have been taken in two consecutive 'fixed' weeks.

| Week 1 | Week 2 | Week 3 | |
|---|---|---|---|
| Rest | Rest | Rest | Rest |
| 45 hours | 24 hours | 27 hours | 45 hours |

CPC Drivers Training Manual

The following table is an example of how the driver's duties might be organised in compliance with the rules on weekly rest, whereby one reduced weekly rest period may be taken in any period of two consecutive weeks under 'normal' circumstances.

| Week 1 | Week 2 | Week 3 |
|---|---|---|
| Rest | Rest | Rest |
| 45 hours | 24 hours | 45 hours |

A weekly rest period that falls in 2 weeks may be counted in either week but not in both. However, where such a rest period is of at least 69 hours in total and starts in one fixed week and ends in the next fixed week, it may be counted as 2 back-to-back weekly rests (eg a 45-hour weekly rest followed by 24 hours), provided that no more than 144 hours (6 x 24 hours) has elapsed since the end of the previous weekly rest period and start of the following weekly rest period.

Where reduced weekly rest periods are taken away from base, these may be taken in a vehicle, provided that it has suitable sleeping facilities and is stationary.

Suitable sleeping facilities - we consider suitable sleeping facilities to be a bunk or other type of bed which is primarily designed for sleeping on. Sleeping on or across seats does not meet the requirement of suitable facilities. If a vehicle has no suitable sleeping facilities then other arrangements, for example guest house or hotel accommodation, should be used.

Note: Operators who utilise a cyclical shift pattern should take care that their shift patterns allow for compliance with the rolling two-weekly requirements for weekly rest and compensation.

## Being on call during a weekly rest period

Drivers who are on call during any period of legally required rest must at all times be able to dispose of the rest time as they choose. This means that an employer cannot impose any limitations on drivers during such periods, for example requiring them to remain in or close to home or at another location. Drivers must be able to dispose of their free time as they choose (but this does not include undertaking any work where they are under the control of or are fulfilling an obligation to an employer). Being on call may only extend as far as a driver

CPC Drivers Training Manual

agreeing to answer a call during a rest period but only if the driver so chooses. On receiving a call to return to work drivers may only do so if they have completed the legally required amount of rest or if the work is deemed to be an emergency. see <u>Emergencies</u>.

# Emergencies

The EU rules do not define an 'emergency' but we consider this would certainly include any of the situations that would be considered an emergency for the purposes of the GB domestic drivers' hours legislation, namely:

- danger to the life or health of people or animals
- serious interruption of essential public services (gas, water, electricity or drainage), of telecommunication and postal services, or in the use of roads, railways, ports or airports
- serious damage to property

Vehicles used in connection with emergency or rescue operations would be exempt from the EU rules for the duration of the emergency. However drivers who have interrupted a rest period to attend an emergency would be required to commence/complete a qualifying rest period before recommencing work.

## Travelling time

Drivers of goods vehicles are sometimes required to travel to a vehicle they are required to drive or from a vehicle they have driven.

Where a vehicle coming within the scope of the EU rules is neither at the driver's home nor at the employer's operational centre where the driver is normally based, but is at a separate location, time spent travelling to or from that location to take charge of the vehicle, regardless of the mode of transport, cannot be counted as a rest or break, unless the driver is in a ferry or train and has access to a bunk or couchette. Even if the driver is not paid or makes the decision themselves to travel to or from home/base the travel time cannot be counted as rest or break.

For example: If a driver had to drive for 1 hour by car to pick up a vehicle from a location that was not the driver's home or their normal operating base then this driving would count as other work. Similarly, if they had to drive back by car from a location that was not their normal operating base, this would count as other work.

CPC Drivers Training Manual

| 1 hr Driving car | 4.5 hrs | 4 hrs | 4 hrs | 30 mins Driving car | Daily or weekly rest |
|---|---|---|---|---|---|

## Unforeseen events

Provided that road safety is not jeopardised, and to enable a driver to reach a suitable stopping place, a departure from the EU rules may be permitted to the extent necessary to ensure the safety of persons, the vehicle or its load. Drivers must note all the reasons for doing so on the back of their tachograph record sheets (if using an analogue tachograph) or on a printout or temporary sheet (if using a digital tachograph) at the latest on reaching the suitable stopping place (see relevant sections covering manual entries). Repeated and regular occurrences, however, might indicate to enforcement officers that employers were not in fact scheduling work to enable compliance with the applicable rules.

A judgment by the European Court of Justice dated 9 November 1995 provides a useful guide to how this provision should be interpreted. It can apply only in cases where it unexpectedly becomes impossible to comply with the rules on drivers' hours during the course of a journey.

In other words, planned breaches of the rules are not allowed. This means that when an unforeseen event occurs, it would be for the driver to decide whether it was necessary to depart from the rules. In doing so, a driver would have to take into account the need to ensure road safety in the process (eg when driving a vehicle carrying an abnormal load under the Special Types regulations) and any instruction that may be given by an enforcement officer (eg when under police escort).

Some examples of such events are delays caused by severe weather, road traffic accidents, mechanical breakdowns, interruptions of ferry services and any event that causes or is likely to cause danger to the life or health of people or animals. Note that this concession only allows for drivers to reach a suitable stopping place, not necessarily to complete their planned journey. Drivers and operators would be expected to reschedule any disrupted work to remain in compliance with the EU rules.

## Summary of EU limits on drivers' hours

The current limits on drivers' hours as specified by the EU rules are summarised below.

## Breaks from driving

A break of no less than 45 minutes must be taken after no more than 4.5 hours of driving. The break can be divided into 2 periods - the first at least 15 minutes long and the second at least 30 minutes - taken over the 4.5 hours.

## Daily driving

Maximum of 9 hours, extendable to 10 hours no more than twice a week.

## Weekly driving

Maximum of 56 hours.

## Two-weekly driving

Maximum of 90 hours in any 2 week period.

## Daily rest

Minimum of 11 hours, which can be reduced to a minimum of 9 hours no more than 3 times between weekly rests. May be taken in 2 periods, the first at least 3 hours long and the second at least 9 hours long. The rest must be completed within 24 hours of the end of the last daily or weekly rest period.

## Multi-manning daily rest

A 9-hour daily rest must be taken within a period of 30 hours that starts from the end of the last daily or weekly rest period. For the first hour of multi-manning, the presence of another driver is optional, but for the remaining time is compulsory.

## Ferry/train daily rest

A regular daily rest period (of at least 11 hours) may be interrupted no more than twice by other activities of not more than 1 hour's duration in total, provided that the driver is accompanying a vehicle that is travelling by ferry or train and has access to a bunk or couchette.

## Weekly rest

A regular weekly rest of at least 45 hours, or reduced weekly rest of a least 24 hours, must be started no later than the end of a 6 consecutive 24-hour period from the end of the last weekly rest. In any 2 consecutive weeks a driver must have at least 2 weekly rests - one of which must be at least 45 hours long. A weekly rest that falls across 2 weeks may be counted in either week but not both. Any reductions must be compensated in one block by an equivalent rest added to another rest period of at least 9 hours before the end of the third week following the week in question.

## AETR rules

Journeys to or through the countries that are signatories to the AETR Agreement see list EU, AETR and EEA countries are subject to AETR rules. AETR rules apply to the whole journey, including any EU countries passed through.

The AETR rules are the same as the EU rules. The same exemptions that apply to EU journeys also apply to AETR journeys – see Exemptions.

For more information refer to the AETR agreement.

CPC Drivers Training Manual

# Working Time Regulations

Drivers who are subject to the EU rules on drivers' hours and tachographs normally have also to comply with the rules on working time as laid out in the Road Transport (Working Time) Regulations, which were brought into force on 4 April 2005. (For the main provisions, see Annex 2. )

## 2. Great Britain domestic rules

How the drivers' hours Great Britain domestic rules work for goods vehicles.

# Overview

The Great Britain domestic rules, as contained in the Transport Act 1968, apply to most goods vehicles that are exempt from the EU rules. Separate rules apply to Northern Ireland.

# Domestic rules exemptions

The following groups are exempt from the domestic drivers' hours rules:

- drivers of vehicles used by the Armed Forces, the police and fire brigade
- drivers who always drive off the public road system
- private driving, ie not in connection with a job or in any way to earn a living

# Domestic driving limits

Driving is defined as being at the controls of a vehicle for the purposes of controlling its movement, whether it is moving or stationary with the engine running, even for a short period of time.

## Daily driving

In any working day the maximum amount of driving permitted is 10 hours. The daily driving limit applies to driving on and off the public road. Off-road driving for the purposes of agriculture, quarrying, forestry, building work or civil engineering counts as duty rather than driving time.

Day: The day is the 24-hour period beginning with the start of duty time.

## Daily duty

In any working day the maximum amount of duty permitted is 11 hours. A driver is exempt from the daily duty limit (11 hours) on any working day when they do not drive.

A driver who does not drive for more than 4 hours on each day of the week is exempt from the daily duty limit for the whole week.

Week: Is the period from 0000 hrs on a Monday to 2400 hrs the following Sunday.

Duty: In the case of an employee driver, this means being on duty (whether driving or otherwise) for anyone who employs them as a driver. This includes all periods of work and driving, but does not include rest or breaks. Employers should also remember that they have additional obligations to ensure that drivers receive adequate rest under health and safety legislation.

For owner drivers, this means driving a vehicle connected with their business, or doing any other work connected with the vehicle and its load.

Drivers of certain vehicles are exempt from the duty but not the driving limit, namely – goods vehicles, including dual purpose vehicles, not exceeding a maximum permitted gross weight of 3.5 tonnes, when used:

- by doctors, dentists, nurses, midwives or vets
- for any service of inspection, cleaning, maintenance, repair, installation or fitting

- by commercial travellers when carrying goods (other than personal effects) only for the purpose of soliciting orders
- by the AA, RAC or RSAC
- for cinematography or radio and television broadcasting

# Record keeping

You must keep written records of your hours of work on a weekly record sheet if you are the driver of a goods vehicle that requires an Operator Licence and you drive for more than 4 hours in that day. An example of such a sheet is at Annex 3. Operators are expected to check and sign each weekly record sheet.

Suppliers of record books containing weekly record sheets can be found on the internet.

Alternatively, an EU-approved and sealed tachograph may be used to record a driver's activities while they are subject to domestic drivers' hours rules. When recording in this manner, and where domestic records are legally required (see flowchart below), all rules on the fitment and use of the tachograph must be complied with see Section 4

Where a tachograph is fitted to a vehicle subject to the domestic rules but is not used to produce a legally required record, the operator and driver should nevertheless ensure that the tachograph is properly calibrated and sealed. The tachograph does not have to be recalibrated provided the seals remain intact and the vehicle remains out of scope of the EU rules.

**Exemptions from keeping records**

Some groups are exempt from requirements to keep records under domestic rules on drivers' hours.

# Emergencies

The GB domestic rules are relaxed in cases where immediate preventative action is needed to avoid:

- danger to the life or health of people or animals
- serious interruption of essential public services (gas, water, electricity or drainage), of telecommunication or postal services, or in the use of roads, railways, ports or airports
- serious damage to property

In these cases the driving and duty limits are suspended for the duration of the emergency.

## Records for vehicles carrying postal articles

Tachographs must be fitted and used on all vehicles with a permissible maximum weight in excess of 3.5 tonnes that carry parcels and letters on postal services. Drivers of such vehicles may be exempt from the EU rules on drivers' hours (see <u>EU rules exemptions</u>) but, if so, must still comply with the GB domestic rules.

## Travelling abroad

The GB domestic rules apply only in GB, but you must observe the national rules of the countries in which you travel. The embassies of these countries will be able to assist in establishing the rules that might apply.

For example, German national rules require drivers of goods vehicles between 2.8 and 3.5 tonnes to record details of their journeys in an AETR-style log book. This means that UK drivers have to use the log book when they set out and while driving through the countries on journeys to or through Germany.

## Mixed vehicle types

If it occurs that a driver divides their time driving goods vehicles and passenger vehicles under GB domestic rules, then in any working day or week, if they spend most of their time driving passenger vehicles then the appropriate GB rules for passenger vehicles apply for that day or week.

## Working Time Regulations

Drivers who are subject to the UK domestic rules on drivers' hours are affected by four provisions under GB Working Time Regulations 1998 (as amended).

CPC Drivers Training Manual

## 3. Mixed EU/AETR and Great Britain domestic driving

How the drivers' hours rules work when you're driving a goods vehicle under a mix of the EU and Great Britain rules.

## Overview

Many drivers spend some of their time driving under one set of rules and some under another set, perhaps even on the same day.

If you work partly under EU/ AETR rules and partly under GB domestic rules during a day or a week, the following points must be considered (the EU rules take precedence over the GB domestic rules):

the time you spend driving or on duty under EU/ AETR rules cannot count as a break or rest period under GB domestic rules

driving and other duty under GB domestic rules (including non-driving work in another employment) count as other work but not as a break or rest period under EU/ AETR rules

driving or other duty under EU/ AETR rules count towards the driving and duty limits under GB domestic rules

any driving under EU/ AETR rules in a week means that you must take a daily rest period on those days when you actually drive under EU/ AETR rules, as well as a weekly rest period

## Driving limits

GB domestic limit (a maximum of 10 hours of driving a day) must always be obeyed. But at any time when you are actually driving under the EU/ AETR rules you must obey all the rules on EU driving limits.

## Other duty limits

GB domestic limit (ie no more than 11 hours on duty) must always be obeyed. But when working under EU/ AETR rules you must also obey all the rules on breaks, daily rest (only on those days when actually driving) and weekly rest.

## Rest periods and breaks

Again, you must always obey the EU/ AETR rules on rest periods and breaks on days and weeks in which driving in scope of EU/ AETR rules is carried out.

A weekly rest period is not required in a fixed week where a driver does not drive under EU/ AETR rules.

Where a driver works under EU/ AETR rules in week one and under GB domestic rules in week two, the driver may take either a regular or a reduced weekly rest in the first week.

If the driver takes a reduced weekly rest, compensation will be required by the end of the third week following the week in question. If this working pattern continues, the driver may take either a regular or reduced weekly rest period every other week.

Where a driver works under GB domestic rules in week one and the EU/ AETR rules in the second week, the weekly rest required in week two must start no later than 144 hours (6 x 24 hours periods) following the commencement of duty on or after 00.00 hours on Monday.

## Records

On any day where both EC/ AETR and GB domestic driving take place then records must be kept in accordance with EC/ AETR requirements, recording any GB domestic work in accordance with the principles set out at the start of this section. Additionally if any 'other work' takes place but prior to any EC or GB domestic driving since the last daily or weekly rest period (taken in accordance with either the EU drivers' hours or working time rules) this must be recorded as 'other work' on a tachograph chart, printout or a manual entry using the manual input facility of a digital tachograph.

'Other work' means all activities which are defined as working time in Article 3(a) of Directive 2002/15/EC except 'driving', including any work for the same or another employer, within or outside of the transport sector.

You must be able to produce such record(s) and any other EC/ AETR records, including your driver card, for the current day and for day when EC/ AETR driving has taken place in the previous 28 calendar days. On a day where only one type of driving takes place (either EU/ AETR or GB domestic) then you should refer to the particular record keeping requirements detailed in the relevant section of this booklet.

## 4. Tachograph rules

The rules about the tachograph that you must use to record your EC/AETR drivers' hours in a goods vehicle.

If the UK leaves the EU without a deal, the EU drivers' hours and tachograph rules will be kept as UK law.

## Overview

You must use an approved tachograph when driving under EU or AETR drivers' hours rules.

The only exception is if you're driving a vehicle collecting sea coal. You'll still have to follow the EU drivers' hours rules, but you don't need a tachograph.

The tachograph is a device that records:

- how many hours you've driven for
- breaks and rest periods
- the vehicle's speed

- the distance the vehicle has travelled

The resulting record is to be used to monitor compliance with rules and drivers' hours.

There are 2 main types of tachograph:

- analogue
- digital (fitted in vehicles registered from 1 May 2006)

The rules on using the tachograph are contained in Regulation (EU) 165/201 and will depend on which of these types you have. These rules must be observed by both drivers and operators of vehicles that fall within the scope of Regulation (EC) 561/2006 or the AETR rules.

**Not in scope?**

The driver of a vehicle that is exempt from or not in scope of the EU rules is not required to use recording equipment, even if it is fitted, unless the vehicle is operated by a universal service provider (USP). At the time of publication, the only USP is the Royal Mail.

## Analogue tachographs

Analogue tachograph recordings are made by a stylus cutting traces into a wax-coated chart. Three separate styluses mark recordings of:

- speed
- distance travelled
- the driver's activity (known as the 'mode')

The inner part is used by the driver to write details of their name, location of start of journey, end location, date and odometer readings.

The reverse of a tachograph chart normally contains an area for recording manual entries and details of other vehicles driven during the period covered.

## Charts and records

Drivers are responsible for operating the tachograph correctly in order to record their activities accurately and fully. Specifically, drivers must:

- verify, before using an instrument, that it is correctly calibrated via the attached plaques and ensure that the time displayed is set to the official time of the country in which the vehicle is registered
- ensure that the correct type of chart is being used for the specific model of tachograph in use
- carry enough charts for the whole journey, including spare charts in case any become damaged or dirty
- enter centrefield details at the first use of the chart, when changing vehicles and when completing the use of the chart (see 'Centrefield entries' section)
- correctly operate the mode switch in order to record their activities accurately see Common rules
- use a second chart if a chart is damaged while in use and attach this one to the first chart on completion - there are other occasions when use of a second chart in a 24-hour period is unavoidable, namely when a driver changes to a vehicle with an incompatible tachograph to the chart in use or they change vehicle so many times that all the details cannot be accommodated on one chart
- make manual entries on the chart in respect of their activities away from the vehicle (see 'Manual entries' section), where the rules have been exceeded in an emergency, or to correct a recording

- make manual entries when the equipment malfunctions and report any such malfunctions to the operator or employer
- not use a chart to cover a period longer than 24 hours
- not remove the chart from the instrument before the end of their duty period unless authorised to do so. The rules do not specify who can authorise removal of the chart, but cases where charts can be removed include:
    - a change of vehicle
    - swapping charts or cards on multi-manned journeys
    - to make manual entries in the event of an emergency, equipment malfunction etc
- return used charts to the operator within 42 days. This requirement must be complied with even when a driver changes employer
- be able to produce at the roadside:
    - charts and any legally required manual records for the current day and the previous 28 calendar days
    - the driver's digital smart card if they hold one
- permit a DVSA examiner or police officer to examine the tachograph instrument and inspect charts

**Time tips**

Make sure the time is correct for am or pm – both times are displayed identically on an analogue tachograph's 12-hour clock face. Analogue tachographs must continue to display the correct time – which for the UK includes adjustments for British Summer Time.

**Activity record**

Most analogue tachograph instruments in use are 'automatic'. This means that the instrument will automatically record activity as driving when the vehicle is moving however it defaults to the selected mode switch setting when the vehicle stops so drivers need to ensure it is set to the appropriate mode for the activity being carried out when the vehicle is stationary.

**Driver cards**

Drivers who have been issued with a driver card are committing an offence if they are unable to produce this during a roadside inspection, even if they only drive analogue tachograph-equipped vehicles.

## Centrefield entries

A driver is required to enter the following information on the centrefield of a tachograph chart that they are using to record their activities:

- surname and first name (the law does not stipulate which order the names are put in – but your employer may have a policy on this)
- the date and place (nearest town or city) where the use of the chart begins and ends. The year may be written in full or abbreviated – so both '2015' and '15' are acceptable - if the start and finish places are the same, both must be written on the chart – ditto marks are not acceptable
- the registration number(s) of vehicle(s) driven (which should be entered before departing on a new vehicle)
- the time at which any change of vehicle takes place
- the odometer readings:
    - at the start of the first journey
    - at the end of the last journey
    - at the time of any change of vehicle, recording the readings from both vehicles

Note that the 'total km' field does not have to be completed.

It is not acceptable for written entries to extend outside the centrefield area if they might interfere with chart recordings. If, for example, the driver's name or a place name is so long it must be abbreviated in order to avoid any possible interference with the recordings, the full name should be noted on the reverse of the chart.

Tachograph charts are required to provide space on their reverse side to record the additional information required in connection with changes of vehicles.

## Manual entries

Drivers must produce a record of their whole daily working period. So when drivers are unable to operate the instrument, have not been allocated a vehicle, or are working away from the vehicle and have had to remove their tachograph chart, they must manually record their activities on the chart.

Manual entries may also be needed at other times – for example, if the tachograph develops a fault, or in the event of an emergency see 'Unforeseen events'. Employers may also ask drivers to indicate on a chart where their duty (or rest) begins and ends, so that they can ensure that a full record has been submitted.

Most analogue charts have a specified place to make manual entries (usually on the reverse) however, manual entries can be made anywhere on the chart provided that they are clear and do not obliterate other recordings.

The following are examples of manual records.

CPC Drivers Training Manual

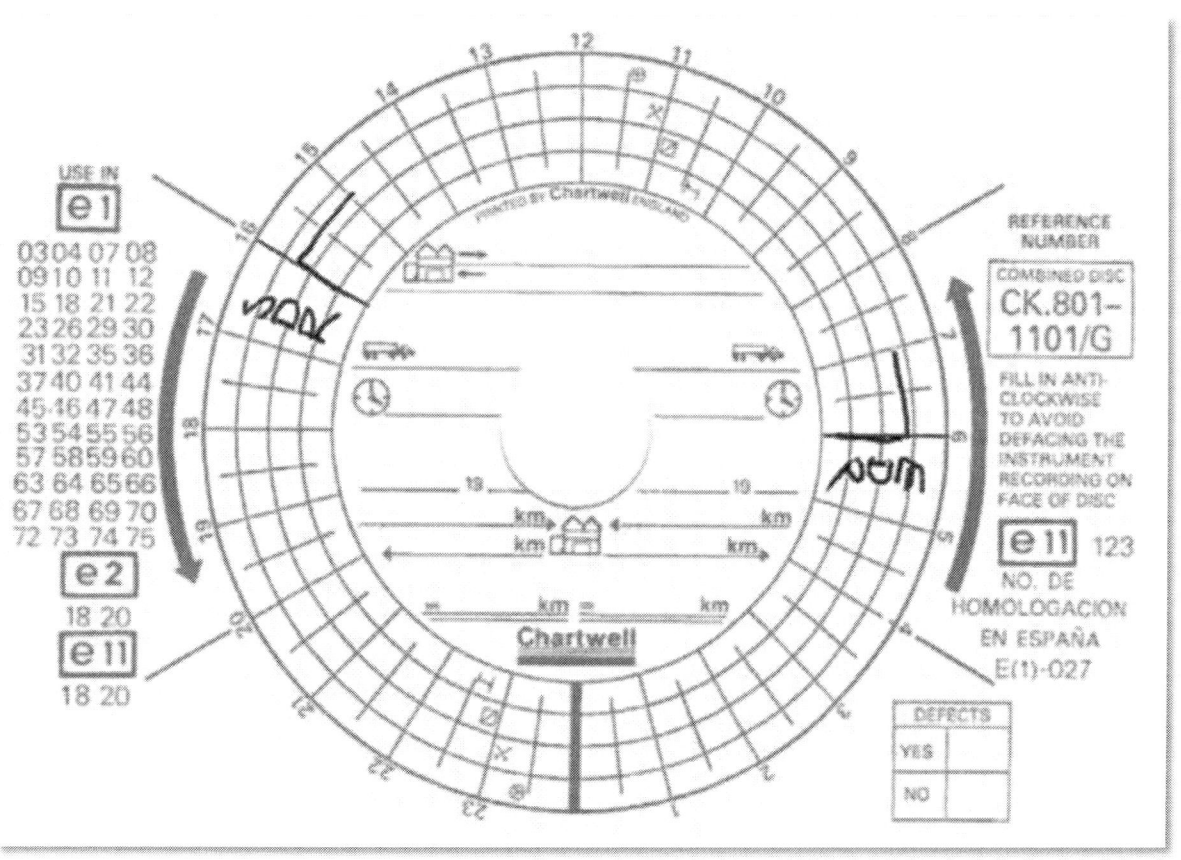

CPC Drivers Training Manual

This is an example of manual entries made on the rear of a tachograph chart of a driver who started their day at 06.00 with an hour's work doing other duties away from their vehicle. They also finished their day with an hour of other work away from their vehicle and have indicated both the end and the start of a daily rest period. Their activities while with the vehicle are recorded by the instrument on the other side of the chart once it has been inserted.

CPC Drivers Training Manual

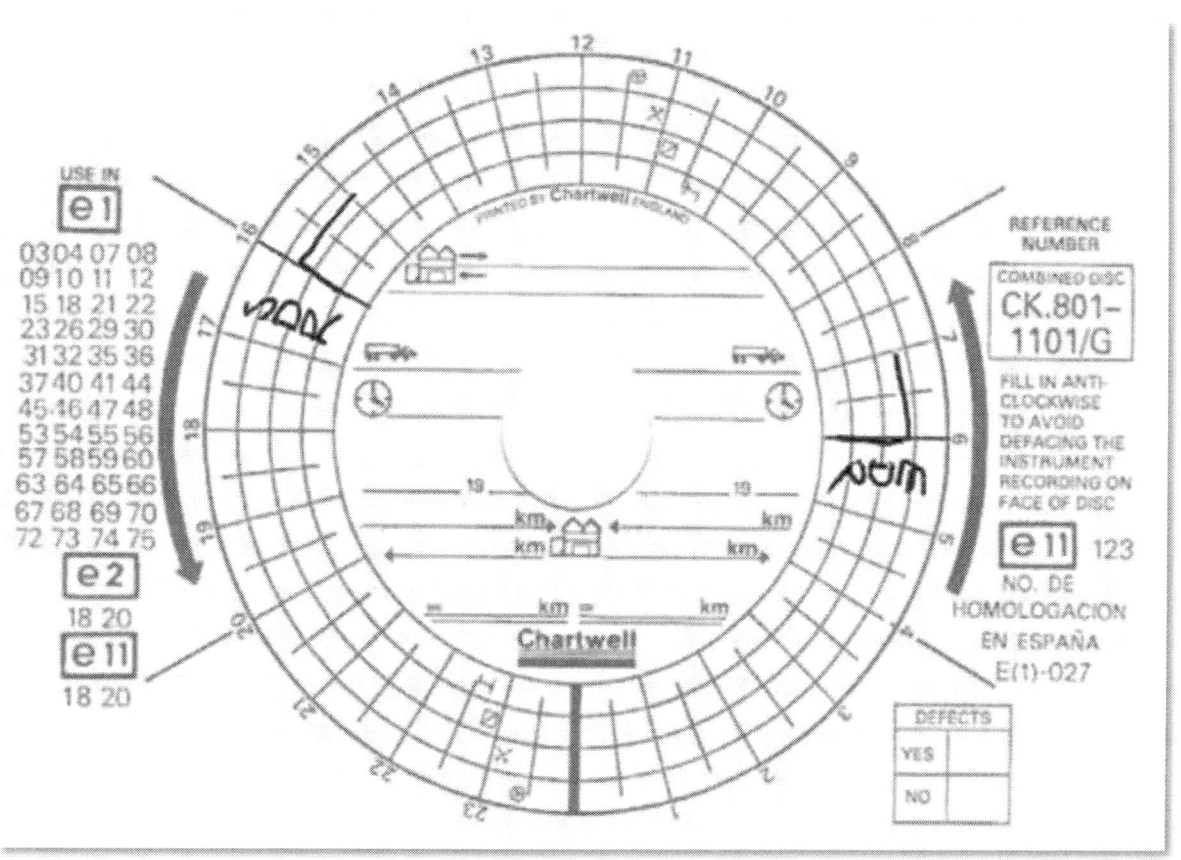

CPC Drivers Training Manual

This is an example of the manual entries made by a driver who changed vehicles at 12.00 in London and continued their duties before finishing in Bristol. All the details of their activities and their name are listed on the other side of the chart.

CPC Drivers Training Manual

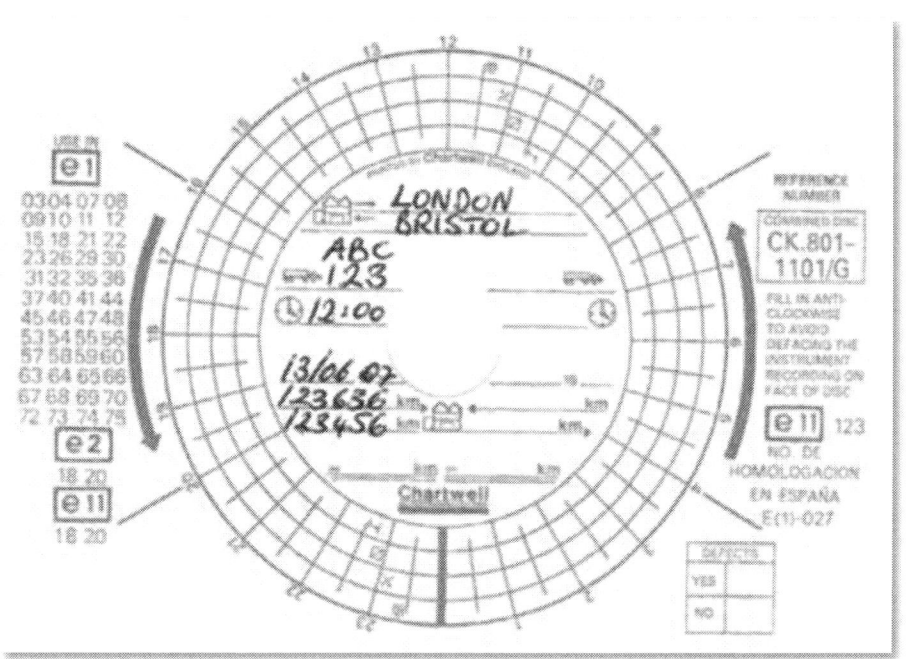

CPC Drivers Training Manual

This is an example of the manual entries that could have been made by a driver who discovered a tachograph fault at 12.00. They use the preprinted matrix to indicate their activities for the remainder of their duty until 18.30. They have also noted the reason for them keeping a manual record. All other details are provided on the other side of the chart.

CPC Drivers Training Manual

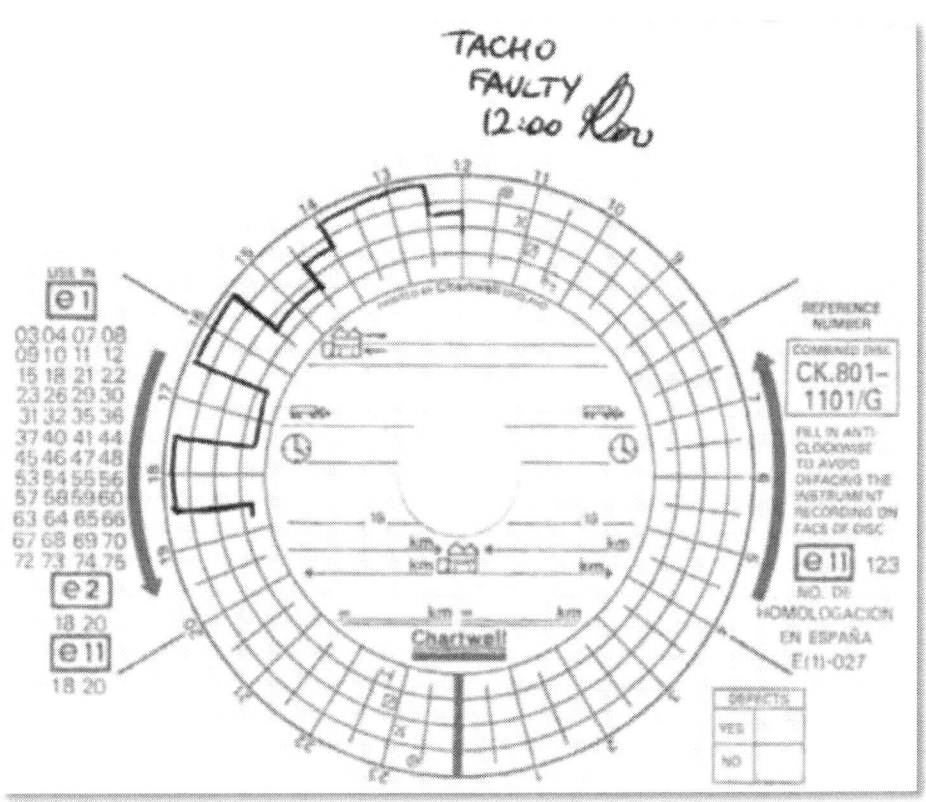

# Digital tachographs

Digital tachographs work by storing digital data on the driver and vehicle in their own memory and separately on a driver's smart card. Transport undertakings must periodically download this data from the digital tachograph (known as the Vehicle Unit or VU) every 90 days and from driver cards every 28 days and analyse the information to ensure that the rules have been complied with.

When driving a vehicle fitted with a digital tachograph on a journey that is not in scope of EU/AETR rules it is recommended, but not legally required, to select 'out-of-scope' in the tachograph. Details of how to do this will be contained in the user manual for the model of tachograph.

## Driver cards and records

It is a legal requirement for a digital tachograph-equipped vehicle driven in scope of EU rules that the driver must use a driver card.

If the vehicle is used without a card being inserted, the system will not prevent the vehicle from being driven, but the VU will record the fact that the vehicle has been used without a card.

Drivers may only be in possession of one driver's smart card, and must never use anyone else's card or allow another driver to use their card.

Drivers must inform the DVLA if their card bears incorrect details, for example after a change of name.

When driving a vehicle that is equipped with a digital tachograph, drivers should:

- ensure that the instrument is calibrated by inspecting the calibration plaque or interrogating the instrument
- ensure that their driver card is inserted into the correct slot (driver in slot 1, second driver in slot 2 from the moment they take over the vehicle, and that it is ready for use, before the vehicle is moved
- record the country in which they begin and end their daily work period. This must always be carried out at the time of the start or end of the period, even if the card is not to be withdrawn or inserted (for example if the card is left in overnight)

# CPC Drivers Training Manual

- carry sufficient supplies of type-approved print roll on board the vehicle so that a printout can be produced at an enforcement officer's request
- ensure that all duties conducted since the driver card was last removed from a tachograph are manually entered onto the card record, using the manual entry facility on the tachograph
- ensure that the tachograph is working properly
- ensure that through the daily working period the mode button is used correctly to record other work, periods of availability, and rest and breaks
- take reasonable steps to protect their card from dirt and damage
- use only their own personalised driver card to record driving and other activities they undertake
- ensure that the card is not removed from the tachograph during the working day unless otherwise authorised. The rules are not specific on who can authorise removal of the card, but cases where cards can be removed include a change of vehicle, or where another driver will be using the vehicle during a break or rest period
- on multi-manning operations ensure that their driver card is placed in the correct slot (slot 1 when they are acting as driver and slot 2 when co-driver on a double-manned journey) when they take over driving
- make their cards available for downloading by their employer
- be able to produce at the roadside:

- - charts and any legally required manual records for the current day and the previous 28 calendar days
  - the driver's digital smart card if they hold one
- sign a hard copy of data when required to do so by a DVSA examiner or a police officer

Mode switch default: Depending on the preferences entered into the digital tachograph at the time of calibration the digital tachograph can default to recording either 'rest' for driver 1 and driver 2 or 'other work' for driver 1 and 'availability' for driver 2 when the vehicle stops. Drivers must use the mode switch correctly to ensure that rest and break periods are recorded correctly.

CPC Drivers Training Manual

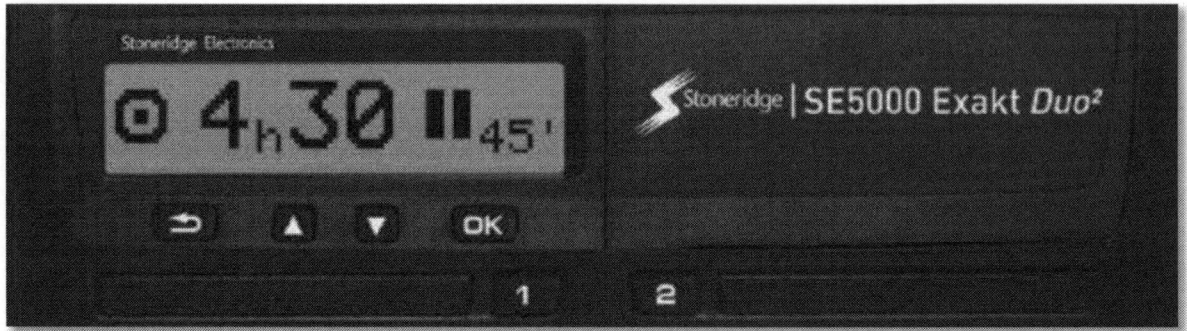

## How to apply for driver cards

You can get application forms and assistance from the Driver and Vehicle Licensing Agency (DVLA) by calling 0300 790 6109. Forms are available to order online at www.dvla.gov.uk. DVLA will accept payment for up to 25 driver card applications on one company cheque.

In Northern Ireland, application forms are available from Driver and Vehicle Licensing Northern Ireland (DVLNI) (call 028 7034 1589) and test centres of the Driver and Vehicle Agency (DVA).

## Lost, stolen or malfunctioning driver cards

Digital tachograph cards have passed all relevant International Organization for Standardization (ISO) qualified tests and security certification requirements. They are designed to work reliably and securely for their period of validity but, like all smart cards, can be damaged by abuse. Take care of your driver card – treat it as if it were a credit card and do not subject it to excessive force, bending or extremes of temperature.

Where it is impossible to use a driver card (e.g. where it has been lost, stolen or damaged or is malfunctioning) a driver may drive without the card for a maximum of 15 calendar days (or longer if this is necessary for the vehicle to be returned to its premises) provided that they produce 2 printouts – one at the start of the day and another at the end so long as there is no change of vehicle. Where there is a change of vehicle then a printout will need to be taken at the start and end of the use of vehicle 1 and then a printout at the start and end of vehicle 2 and so on. All printouts must be marked with:

- the driver's name or driver card or licence number, so the driver can be identified
- any manual entries needed to show periods of other work, availability, and rest or break
- the driver's signature

CPC Drivers Training Manual

The driver must report the problem to DVLA and apply for a new card within seven calendar days.

## UTC – the time set on a digital tachograph

The internal clock of a digital tachograph is set to Universal Time Co-ordinated (UTC). The time displayed on the clock face can be set by the driver either to local time or to UTC. However, all data will be recorded by the VU on the time set by the integral clock, which operates on UTC – this is the same as Greenwich Mean Time (GMT). You will need to remember that UTC is one hour behind British Summer Time (BST). So, between 01.00 on the last Sunday in March and 01.00 on the last Sunday in October drivers must account for the difference when manually inputting activity details in the digital tachograph.

For example, if drivers carried out other work for two hours between 06.00 and 08.00 in June before taking over the vehicle, they must enter this as between 05.00 and 07.00 in UTC time. As mentioned above, it is possible for drivers to set the display time on the VU to local BST, but this will not prevent the VU recording in UTC. Therefore, it is recommended that drivers leave the display time in UTC as a reminder of the difference.

## Manual records

A digital tachograph offers the ability for a driver to enter activities carried out by them away from their vehicle. This is by means of the manual input facility offered by the instrument. There is however no requirement to make a manual record on a driver card where all the activity has already been captured on an analogue record sheet.

Analogue tachographs do not have a manual input facility so a manual record must be made on the reverse of the record sheet detailing the type of activity and the times started and finished. further details are given in the section relating to analogue tachographs under the heading of 'manual records'.

# CPC Drivers Training Manual

The only time a manual record or entry is legally required is when:

| Reason | Action |
|---|---|
| Activity takes place away from the vehicle and is not possible to use the recording equipment. | Manual record to be kept on analogue record sheet, on printout paper or by manual input on a digital tachograph where possible. |
| The equipment or card malfunctions. | Manual record must be kept on an analogue record sheet or on printout paper. |
| The rules are breached due to an unforeseen event (see page 19). | Record reasons on a printout or the reverse of a portion of print roll, at the latest on arrival at the suitable stopping place. |
| A record needs to be corrected because the incorrect mode has been recorded | Amend record, including the reason, on a printout or the reverse of a portion of print roll as soon as possible. |

Manual records must be kept and produced in the same way as any other record which has been produced using recording equipment.

# Common rules

## Operation of the mode switch or button

Drivers must ensure that the mode switch on an analogue tachograph or the mode button on a digital tachograph is correctly set to record their activities.

| Symbol | Explanatory note |
|---|---|
| Driving symbol | This is automatically recorded on most tachographs. |
| Other work | Covers all activities defined as work other than driving in scope of EU/ AETR rules. Includes any work for the same or another employer, within or outside the transport sector |
| Availability | Covers periods of waiting time, the duration of which is known about in advance. Examples of what might count as a period of availability (POA) are accompanying a vehicle on a ferry crossing or waiting while other workers |

| Symbol | Explanatory note |
|---|---|
|  | load/unload your vehicle. For mobile workers driving in a team, a POA would also include time spent sitting next to the driver while the vehicle is in motion (unless taking a break or performing other work, ie navigation) |
| Break or rest | Covers breaks in work and daily or weekly rest periods. Drivers may not carry out any driving or any other work. Break periods are to be used exclusively for recuperation. During a rest period a driver must be able to dispose freely of their time. |

If for any reason the tachograph does not make an accurate record of activities (eg if the driver inadvertently makes an incorrect manual entry in a digital tachograph, or fails to correctly operate the mode button or switch), it is strongly recommended that the driver makes a manual tachograph record to this effect. For digital equipment, the driver should make and sign a printout for the relevant period with a note giving details of the error and reason at the time the error is made. For analogue equipment, the record should be made at the back of the chart.

## Multi-manning – second driver record

Some analogue equipment and all digital tachographs will automatically record all time spent as a second driver when the vehicle is in motion as a period of availability and do not allow the mode to be changed to either 'break' or 'other work'. Provided the second driver is not required to carry out any work during this time, enforcement authorities will accept the first 45 minutes of this time as a break from driving. Any periods of other work, however, must be manually recorded on a printout or chart by the driver.

## Travelling time

In cases where a vehicle that comes within the scope of EU rules is at a separate location that is neither the driver's home nor the employer's operational centre where the driver is normally based, but is at a separate location, the time the driver spends travelling to or from that location to take charge of that vehicle, regardless of the mode of transport, cannot be counted as a rest or break, unless the driver is in a ferry or train and has access to a bunk or couchette. Even if the driver is not paid or makes the decision themselves to travel to or from home/ base the travel time cannot be counted as rest or break. Travelling time must therefore be recorded as "other work" or "availability" in accordance with the above descriptions.

## Mixed records – analogue and digital equipment

It is possible that a driver may, during the course of a day, drive two or more vehicles where both types of recording equipment are used. Drivers in such a situation must use a driver card to record while driving a vehicle with a digital tachograph and tachograph charts when driving a vehicle equipped with an analogue device. Time away from the vehicle may be recorded on either recording equipment, but there is no need to record it on both.

Note: A driver who is not in possession of a driver card cannot drive a vehicle equipped with a digital tachograph.

## Recording other work

During a week in which in-scope driving has taken place, any previous work ( including out-of scope driving) since the last daily or weekly rest period ( taken in accordance with either the EU drivers' hours or working time rules), would have to be recorded as 'other work' on a tachograph chart, printout or manual entry using the manual input facility of a digital tachograph chart, or a legally required GB domestic record on a log book.

'Other work' means all activities which are defined as working time in Article 3(a) of Directive 2002/15/EC except 'driving', including any work for the same or another employer, within or outside of the transport sector.

The record must be either:

- written manually on a chart
- written manually on a printout from a digital tachograph
- made by using the manual input facility of a digital tachograph or
- for days where a driver has been subject to the domestic drivers' hours rules and a record is legally required see Record keeping, recorded in a domestic log book

## Information to operators

A driver who is at the disposal of more than one transport undertaking must provide each undertaking with sufficient information to allow them to make sure the rules are being met.

## Rest and other days off

The period of time unaccounted for between successive charts produced by a driver should normally be regarded as (unless there is evidence to the contrary) a rest period when drivers are able to dispose freely of their time. In the UK, drivers are not expected to account for this period, unless enforcement authorities have reason to believe that they were working. There is no legal requirement to produce an attestation letter but we are currently unaware how other EU Member States view this issue and some may currently require letters of attestation. We would therefore recommend, until the position becomes clear, that drivers carry letters of attestation from the employer for drivers travelling through other countries to cover any sick leave, annual leave and time spent driving a vehicle which is not in scope of EU/ AETR rules during the preceding 28 days.

## Responsibilities of operators

Operators of transport undertakings have legal responsibilities and liabilities for their own compliance with the regulations and that of the drivers under their control. Transport undertakings must:

- ensure that tachographs have been calibrated, inspected and re-calibrated in line with the rules
- supply sufficient quantity of type-approved charts and print roll to drivers
- ensure the return of used tachograph charts from drivers. Note that this responsibility continues after a driver has left employment until all charts are returned
- ensure drivers are properly trained and instructed on the rules relating to drivers' hours and the correct functioning and use of tachograph recording equipment
- properly schedule work so the rules are met
- not make payments to drivers related to distances travelled and/or the amount of goods carried if that would encourage breaches of the rules

**Download data from the vehicle unit**

You must download data from the vehicle unit:

- at least every 90 calendar days
- immediately before transferring control of the use of the vehicle to another person (for example, when the vehicle is sold or un-hired)
- without delay upon permanently removing the unit from service in the vehicle

- without delay upon becoming aware that the unit is malfunctioning, if it is possible to download data
- without delay in any circumstances where it is reasonably foreseeable that data will be erased imminently
- in any case as often as necessary to ensure that no data is lost (the Vehicle Unit holds 365 days' worth of average data, after which the memory is full and the oldest data is overwritten and lost)

**Download data from driver cards**

You must download data from driver cards:

- at least every 28 calendar days
- immediately before the driver ceases to be employed by the undertaking (remember that this also applies to agency drivers)
- without delay upon being aware that the card has been damaged or is malfunctioning, if it is possible to download data
- without delay in any circumstances where it is reasonably foreseeable that data will be erased imminently

- where it is only possible to download the card via a vehicle unit (for example, if the card is stuck), immediately before ceasing control of the use of the vehicle
- in any case as often as necessary to ensure that no data is lost (the driver card holds 28 days of average data, after which the memory is full and the oldest data is overwritten and lost. An average day is deemed to be 93 activity changes. In certain operations where more than 93 activity changes are recorded in a day, a driver card may hold less than 28 days of data)

**Provide copies**

Provide copies of charts and digital data to drivers if requested to do so.

**Regular checks**

Make regular checks of charts and digital data to ensure compliance.

**Produce records**

Be able to produce records to enforcement officers for 12 months.

**Breaches of rules**

Take all reasonable steps to prevent breaches of the rules.

## Tachograph calibration and inspection

All tachographs used for recording drivers' hours, whether analogue or digital, must be properly installed, calibrated and sealed. This task must be performed either by a vehicle manufacturer or an approved tachograph calibration centre (call DVSA on 0300 123 9000 to find your nearest approved tachograph centre). An installation plaque must be fixed to or near the tachograph. Tachograph calibration centres will issue a certificate showing details of any inspection conducted.

Analogue tachographs must be inspected every 2 years and recalibrated every 6 years. Digital tachographs must be recalibrated:

- every 2 years
- after any repair
- if the vehicle registration number changes
- if UTC is out by more than 20 minutes

- after an alteration to the circumference of the tyres or characteristic coefficient

Inspection and recalibration dates are shown on the plaque and updated by calibration centres. Operators must ensure that these tachograph requirements are complied with before a new or used vehicle goes into service.

## Breakdown of equipment

EU legislation requires that in the event of a breakdown or faulty operation of the equipment, it must be repaired as soon as possible. If the vehicle is unable to return to its base within a week the repair must be carried out en route.

GB legislation also provides that a driver or operator will not be liable to be convicted if they can prove to a court that the vehicle was on its way to a place where the recording equipment could be repaired, or that it was not immediately practicable for the equipment to be repaired and the driver was keeping a manual record. Additionally, they will not be liable where a seal is broken and the breaking of the seal was unavoidable and it could not be immediately repaired, providing that all other aspects of the EU rules were being complied with.

For faults and breakdowns involving digital tachographs, operators should ask the repair centre to download any data held on the unit. If this is not possible the centre should issue the operator with a 'certificate of undownloadability', which must be kept for at least 12 months.

International journeys: Although this is the position under EU rules, it is not advisable to start or continue an international journey with a defective tachograph, even if manual records are kept. This is because many countries will not permit entry by such vehicles, since their own domestic laws require a fully functioning system.

## Digital tachographs – company cards

Company cards are issued by DVLA in the company name. Company cards do not primarily hold data but act as an electronic key to protect and access data from the digital tachograph. A company can hold up to 2,232 cards, which will have identical card numbers but different issue numbers at the end of the card number that enable operators to tell them apart.

Company cards are needed to download data from the VU – they can be placed in either driver card slot. Company cards are not needed in order to access information from a driver card where it is being downloaded separately from the VU.

Operators may also use the company card to lock in (in other words, protect) their drivers' details. Once an operator has locked in, all subsequent data is protected and the full details may only be downloaded by inserting the same numbered company card. Locking in is especially recommended since failure to do so could lead to an operator being unable to download its data if the data held in the VU has been protected by a previous operator linking in with its card.

The cards can be used to lock out when they have finished with a vehicle – for example, if it has been sold or if operators have used a hired vehicle. This will signify the end of their interest in the vehicle and its operations, although failing to do this will not prevent another company protecting its own data by locking in, as locking in will automatically lock out the previous protection.

Operators who use hired vehicles may need to train their drivers, and equip them with the means, to download VU data from vehicles at the point of un-hire where this occurs away from base.

Operators can apply for company cards by calling the DVLA at 0300 790 6109 to obtain an application form (form ST2A).

In Northern Ireland, application forms are available from DVA by:

- calling the Driver and Vehicle Licensing Enquiry Section on 0845 402 4000

## 5. Enforcement and penalties

The powers and sanctions available to enforce breaches of drivers' hours for goods vehicles.

If the UK leaves the EU without a deal, the EU drivers' hours and tachograph rules will be kept as UK law.

# Enforcement powers and sanctions

# Powers

Legislation has provided authorised DVSA examiners with powers that include:

- the power to inspect vehicles
- the power to prohibit and direct vehicles
- powers relating to the investigation of possible breaches of regulations and
- the power to instigate, conduct and appear in proceedings at a magistrates' court
- the power to issue improvement notices and prohibition notices in relation to working time rules

# Sanctions

Action taken against drivers' hours and tachograph rules infringements is largely determined by legislation, and includes the following:

## Verbal warnings

Minor infringements that appear to enforcement staff to have been committed either accidentally or due to the inexperience of the driver/operator and are isolated instances may be dealt with by means of a verbal warning. This will include a clarification of the infringement and an explanation of the consequences of continued infringement.

## Offence rectification notice

These may be issued to operators for a number of infringements not related to safety, and give them 21 days to carry out a rectification of the shortcoming, otherwise prosecution will be considered.

## Prohibition

Many drivers' hours and tachograph rules infringements attract a prohibition. A prohibition is not strictly a 'sanction', rather an enforcement tool to remove an immediate threat to road safety. When issued, driving of the vehicle is prohibited for either a specified or an unspecified period until the conditions stated on the prohibition note are satisfied. Where the prohibition is issued for an unspecified period, a note indicating the removal of the prohibition must be issued before use of the vehicle is permitted. In addition to attracting a prohibition, the matter will be considered for prosecution.

In certain circumstances a vehicle which has been prohibited will also be immobilised to prevent further use. Once the situation which led to the prohibition being imposed has been rectified and the payment of a fee has been made the vehicle will be released.

## Fixed penalties and deposits

Infringing drivers with verifiable UK addresses are, in the most routine cases, dealt with by means of a fixed penalty, which can be considered by the driver for up to 28 days. Breaches of drivers' hours rules will attract a level of fixed penalty fine that is graduated depending on the seriousness. Drivers without a verifiable address are asked to pay a deposit equal to the fixed penalty and further driving is prohibited pending receipt of that payment. DVSA can still take cases to court if it is deemed necessary.

## Prosecution

If it is considered to be in the public interest, more serious infringements are considered for prosecution, either against the driver, the operator or other undertakings, or against all of them. (See also EU rules: co-liability on <u>Infringements of the EU drivers' hours rules</u>.

## Referral to the Traffic Commissioner

Where the driver is the holder of a vocational licence and/or the operator is the holder of an operator's licence, enforcement staff may report infringements by either the driver or the operator to the Traffic Commissioner instead of, or as well as, prosecution. This may occur when enforcement staff believe that the matter under consideration brings into doubt the repute of the driver/operator and subsequently call on the Traffic Commissioner to decide whether any administrative action should be taken against their licences.

## Infringements of GB domestic drivers' hours rules

Where an infringement of the domestic drivers' hours rules occurs, the law protects from conviction in court those drivers who can prove that, because of unforeseen difficulties, they were unavoidably delayed in finishing a journey and breached the rules. It also protects employers if any driver was involved in other driving jobs that the employer could not have known about.

## Infringements of the EU drivers' hours rules

The law protects from conviction in court those drivers who can prove that, because of unforeseen difficulties, they were unavoidably delayed in finishing a journey and breached the rules.

The EU rules make transport undertakings liable for any infringements committed by their drivers.

However, transport undertakings will not be held responsible for these offences if they can show that at the time of the infringement the driver's work was being organised in full consideration of the rules, and in particular that:

- no payments were made that encouraged breaches
- work was properly organised
- the driver was properly instructed and
- regular checks were made

Transport undertakings must also show that they have taken all reasonable steps to avoid the contravention. Employers also have a defence if they can prove that the driver was involved in other driving jobs that the employer could not reasonably have known about. Where it is found that an undertaking has failed in its obligations, prosecution may be considered against the undertaking for a driver's offence.

In the case of infringements concerning records, the law protects an employer from conviction if they can prove that they took all reasonable steps to make sure that the driver kept proper records.

Under the EU rules, enforcement action can be taken against operators and drivers for offences detected in Great Britain but committed in another country, provided that the offender has not already been penalised.

To prevent further penalties being imposed for the same offence, enforcement agencies must provide the driver with evidence of the proceedings or penalties in writing. The driver is required to carry the documentation until such time as the infringement cannot lead to further action.

## EU rules: co-liability

The EU rules also make undertakings such as consignors, freight forwarders, tour operators, principal contractors, sub-contractors and driver employment agencies responsible for ensuring that contractually agreed transport time schedules respect the rules on drivers' hours.

The undertaking must take all reasonable steps to comply with this requirement. If a contract with the customer includes a provision for transport time schedules to respect the EU rules, then the requirement would normally be satisfied. However, a driver employment agency is unlikely to absolve itself from the liability if it is found to have been offering back-to-back jobs to drivers where it will be impossible for the driver in question to take a daily or weekly rest in between those jobs.

We consider the term 'driver employment agency' to include employment businesses as defined in the Employment Agencies Act 1973, Section 13(3).

# Penalties for infringements of the drivers' hours rules in Great Britain

## Maximum fines

As contained within Part VI of the Transport Act 1968 (as amended), the maximum fines that can be imposed by a court of law on conviction are as follows:

| Offence | Penalty |
| --- | --- |
| Failure to observe driving times, break or rest period rules | Level 4 fine |
| Failure to make or keep records under the GB rules | Level 4 fine |
| Failure to install a tachograph | Level 5 fine |
| Failure to use a tachograph | Level 5 fine |
| Failure to hand over records relating to recording equipment as requested by an enforcement officer | Level 5 fine |
| False entry or alteration of a record with the intent to | On summary conviction Level 5 fine or |

| Offence | Penalty |
|---|---|
| deceive | on indictment 2 years' imprisonment |
| Altering or forging the seal on a tachograph with the intent to deceive | On summary conviction Level 5 fine or on indictment 2 years' imprisonment |
| Failure to take all reasonable steps to ensure contractually agreed transport time schedules respect the EU rules | Level 4 fine |

# Annex 1. Legislation

The legislation about drivers' hours rules.

If the UK leaves the EU without a deal, the EU drivers' hours and tachograph rules will be kept as UK law.

## EU rules

- EC Regulation 561/2006 on drivers' hours and tachographs
- EU 165/2014 on tachographs and drivers' hours (repealing Council Reg. (EEC) 3821/85 on recording equipment in road transport and amending Reg (EC) 561/2006)
- The Transport Act 1968 (Part VI as amended)
- The Road Traffic (Drivers' Ages and Work) Act 1976
- The Transport Act 1978
- The Community Drivers' Hours and Recording Equipment Regulations 1986 (SI 1986/1457)
- The Drivers' Hours (Harmonisation with Community Rules) Regulations 1986 (SI 1986/1458)

- The Passenger and Goods Vehicles (Recording Equipment) Regulations 1989 (SI 1989/2121)
- The Passenger and Goods Vehicles (Recording Equipment) (Tachograph Card Fees) Regulations 2005 (SI 2005/1140)
- The Passenger and Goods Vehicles (Recording Equipment) Regulations 2005 (SI 2005/1904)
- The Passenger and Goods Vehicles (Recording Equipment) (Tachograph Card) Regulations 2006 (SI 2006/1937)
- The Passenger and Goods Vehicles (Recording Equipment) (Fitting Date) Regulations 2006 (SI 2006/1117)
- The Community Drivers' Hours and Recording Equipment Regulations 2007 (SI 2007/1819)
- The Passenger and Goods Vehicles (Recording Equipment) (Downloading and Retention of Data) Regulations 2008 (SI 2008/198)
- The Passenger and Goods Vehicles (Community Recording Equipment Regulations) 2010 (SI 2010/892)
- The Community Drivers' Hours and Recording Equipment Regulations 2012 (SI 2012/1502)
- The Passenger and Goods Vehicle (Recording Equipment)(Downloading of Data) Regulations 2015 (SI 2015/502)

- The Passenger and Goods Vehicle (Tachographs)(Amendment) Regulations 2016

## AETR rules

- European Agreement Concerning the Work of Crews on Vehicles Engaged in International Road Transport (AETR) (Cm 7401) (as amended by Cmnd 9037)

## Domestic rules

- Transport Act 1968 (Part VI as amended)
- The Drivers' Hours (Goods Vehicles) (Modifications) Order 1970 (SI 1970/257)
- The Drivers' Hours (Passenger and Goods Vehicles) (Modifications) Order 1971 (SI 1971/818)
- The Drivers' Hours (Goods Vehicles) (Modifications) Order 1986 (SI 1986/1459)
- The Drivers' Hours (Goods Vehicles) (Exemptions) Regulations 1986 (SI 1986/1492)
- The Drivers' Hours (Goods Vehicles) (Keeping of Records) Regulations 1987 (SI 1987/1421)
- Drivers' Hours (Harmonisation with Community Rules) Regulations 1986 (SI 1986/1458)

## Annex 2. Working time rules

The working time rules that apply to you depend on whether you drive a vehicle in scope of the EU or GB domestic drivers' hours rules.

## Driving under the EU drivers' hours rules

If you operate a vehicle in scope of the EU drivers' hours rules, then you are subject to the Road Transport (Working Time) Regulations 2005 (as amended – 'the 2005 Regulations'), unless you are an occasional mobile worker (see text boxes at the end of this Annex for definitions).

The main provisions of the 2005 Regulations are as follows:

- weekly working time must not exceed an average of 48 hours per week over the reference period - a maximum working time of 60 hours can be performed in any single week providing the average 48-hour limit is not exceeded
- night work: if night work is performed, working time must not exceed 10 hours in any 24-hour period. Night time is the period between 00.00 and 04.00 for goods vehicles

and between 01.00 and 05.00 for passenger vehicles. The 10-hour limit may be exceeded if this is permitted under a collective or workforce agreement
- breaks:
  - mobile workers must not work more than 6 consecutive hours without taking a break
  - if your working hours total between 6 and 9 hours, working time should be interrupted by a break or breaks totalling at least 30 minutes
  - if your working hours total more than 9 hours, working time should be interrupted by a break or breaks totalling at least 45 minutes
  - breaks should be of at least 15 minutes' duration
- rest: the regulations are the same as the EU or AETR drivers' hours rules
- record keeping: records need to be kept for two years after the period in question

The reference period for calculating the 48-hour week is normally 17 weeks, but it can be extended to 26 weeks if this is permitted under a collective or workforce agreement.

There is no 'opt-out' for individuals wishing to work longer than an average 48-hour week, but breaks and 'periods of availability' do not count as working time.

Generally speaking, a period of availability (POA) is waiting time, the duration of which is known about in advance. Examples of what might count as a POA are accompanying a vehicle on a ferry crossing or waiting while other workers load/unload your vehicle. For mobile workers driving in a team, a POA would also include time spent sitting next to the driver while the vehicle is in motion (unless the mobile worker is taking a break or performing other work ie navigation).

In addition, you are affected by two provisions under the Working Time Regulations 1998 (as amended – 'the 1998 Regulations'). These are:

- an entitlement to 5.6 weeks' paid annual leave
- health checks for night workers

If you only occasionally drive vehicles subject to the EU drivers' hours rules, you may be able to take advantage of the exemption from the 2005 Regulations for occasional mobile workers (see text box below to see if you meet the criteria).

Self-employed drivers were brought in scope of the EU Working Time Directive 2002/15/EC in GB in May 2012, by the Road Transport (Working Time) Amendment Regulations 2012.

CPC Drivers Training Manual

DVSA enforces the provisions of the 2005 Regulations and the requirement for health checks for night workers (under the 1998 Regulations). If you have any questions about matters relating to annual leave, call the Advisory, Conciliation and Arbitration Service (Acas) national helpline on 0300 123 1100, for free support and advice.

## Driving under the GB domestic drivers' hours rules (or are an occasional mobile worker)

If you drive a vehicle subject to the GB domestic drivers' hours rules or are an occasional mobile worker (see text box for definition below), you are affected by four provisions under the 1998 Regulations.

These are:

- weekly working time, which must not exceed an average of 48 hours per week over the reference period (although individuals can 'opt out' of this requirement if they want to)
- an entitlement to 5.6 weeks' paid annual leave
- health checks for night workers
- an entitlement to adequate rest

CPC Drivers Training Manual

**Adequate rest**

Adequate rest means that workers should have regular rest periods. These rest periods should be sufficiently long and continuous to ensure that workers do not harm themselves, fellow workers or others and that they do not damage their health in the short or long term.

The reference period for calculating the 48-hour average week is normally a rolling 17-week period. However, this reference period can be extended up to 52 weeks, if this is permitted under a collective or workforce agreement.

The 1998 Regulations do not apply to self-employed drivers (see text box below for definition). Please note that this definition is different to the one used under the 2005 Regulations.

DVSA enforces the working time limits and the requirement for health checks for night workers under the 1998 Regulations for drivers operating under the GB domestic drivers' hours rules (and occasional mobile workers). If you have any questions about matters relating to rest or annual leave, call the ACAS national helpline on 0300 123 1100, for free support and advice.

# Annex 3. Example Sheet

| Day on which duty commenced | Registration no. of vehicle(s) | Place where vehicle(s) based | Time of going on duty | Time of going off duty | Time spent driving | Time spent on duty | Driver's signature |
|---|---|---|---|---|---|---|---|
| Monday | | | | | | | |
| Tuesday | | | | | | | |
| Wednesday | | | | | | | |
| Thursday | | | | | | | |
| Friday | | | | | | | |
| Saturday | | | | | | | |
| Sunday | | | | | | | |

Driver's name

Period covered by sheet
Week commencing (date) _____
To week ending (date) _____

Certification by employer

I have examined the entries in this sheet
Signature _____
Position held _____

## Further information

For further details on the 1998 Regulations, contact the Department for Business, Innovation and Skills on 020 7215 5000 or access their website at www.bis.gov.uk

## Definition of a self-employed driver under the 2005 Regulations

'Self-employed driver' means anyone whose main occupation is to transport passengers or goods by road for hire or reward within the meaning of Community legislation under cover of a Community licence or any other professional authorisation to carry out such transport, who is entitled to work for himself and who is not tied to an employer by an employment contract or by any other type of working hierarchical relationship, who is free to organise the relevant working activities, whose income depends directly on the profits made and who has the freedom, individually or through a co-operation between self-employed drivers, to have commercial relations with several customers (Regulation 2 of SI 2005/639).

## Definition of an occasional mobile worker under the 2005 Regulations

A mobile worker would be exempt from the 2005 Regulations if:

- they work 10 days or less within scope of the European drivers' hours rules in a reference period that is shorter than 26 weeks or
- they work 15 days or less within scope of the European drivers' hours rules in a reference period that is 26 weeks or longer

CPC Drivers Training Manual

## Definition of self-employed under the 1998 Regulations

You are self-employed if you are running your own business and are free to work for different clients and customers.

Printed in Great Britain
by Amazon